It's
Your
Decision
for Teens

It's
Your
Decision
for Teens

A Commonsense Guide to
Making Better Choices

AL FODERARO
& DENISE SCHMIDT

authorHOUSE®

AuthorHouse™
1663 Liberty Drive
Bloomington, IN 47403
www.authorhouse.com
Phone: 1-800-839-8640

First published by AuthorHouse   10/18/2011

ISBN: 978-1-4634-4823-3 (sc)
ISBN: 978-1-4634-4822-6 (ebk)

Library of Congress Control Number: 2011914177

Printed in the United States of America

CONTENTS

INTRODUCTION: YOUR TEENAGE YEARS

Your teenage years are a bridge between childhood and adulthood. These years are the perfect time for self-assessment, career planning, and personal development. They are years filled with high expectations and great responsibility.

During your teen years, you will be asked to make some very important decisions. What are you going to do after you graduate from high school? What do you want to be when you grow up? Before you can answer these questions, you will want to ask yourself a few other questions. What do you like to do? What are you good at? Consider these kinds of questions before you finish high school and you will be better prepared to make decisions about your life after graduation.

Start Soon

The choices that you make as a teenager will have a significant impact on your life as an adult. Starting the career planning process early in your teens will give you time to gather information about yourself and the opportunities around you. The more effort you put into making good academic and career decisions now, the brighter your future will be.

As you move through your teenage years, you will become less dependent on your parents and other adults. You will begin to make decisions about your future and begin to put your choices into action. First, though, you will need to learn how to make decisions. Once you understand the process, you will be able to start using it in your daily life. It's simple, it's easy, and it works.

Make Your Own Decisions

Teens who do not want to make their own decisions too often rely on others to decide things for them. Unfortunately, others do not always do what is best for us. Make your own decisions and you will be more satisfied and confident in the choices you make. Accept responsibility for making the academic, career, and personal decisions that lie ahead.

Learn How to Make Decisions

It's Your Decision (for Teens) will help you to make decisions the right way—carefully and thoughtfully. During the teenage years, decisions are waiting for you around every corner. You cannot avoid them and you cannot let others make them for you. We are not talking about the very simple decisions you make every day like what to wear or what movie to see. We want to help you make what we call "big-ticket" decisions. Big-ticket decisions are ones that will shape your future. Even now, the decisions you make about what kind of student you are, who your friends are, and what you do in your free time can make a difference in your life.

The decisions that matter most are the ones you make from now on. Be especially careful when you are making big-ticket decisions. Make the right choices now and you will be glad later that you did.

Questions to Think About

1. Do you make your own decisions or do you rely on others to make decisions for you?

2. Who influences you when you are making decisions?

3. Why might letting others make decisions for you have negative consequences?

4. What good decisions have you made in the last year?

5. What bad decisions have you made?

6. What could you have done differently to make the bad decisions, good ones?

Your Thoughts

_____

_____

_____

_____

_____

_____

_____

_____

_____

_____

SOONER THAN YOU THINK

The good news is that as a teenager, you can use the next few years to learn more about yourself and about jobs and careers that you might enjoy later on. By gathering that information now, when the time comes for you to make decisions about your education or about what you want to do when you grow up, you will be able to make choices that are right for you.

Do not make the mistake of thinking that you have plenty of time to do this and put it out of your mind for months or even years. Between now and when you finish high school, you will have lots of chances to do and learn things that will give you even more options later on. Watch for those opportunities and take advantage of them because sooner than you think, you are going to have to make decisions and choices that will begin to shape your life.

Stay on Track

It is important to keep your future in mind as you move from grade to grade. Think about who you are, how you are changing, and what that means when it comes to going to college or to work after high school. You may want to use a checklist, like the one that follows, as a guide. It will help you to keep track of what you have done and what you need to do to be able to make those choices. Record your accomplishments and watch your progress. See what you have done and make plans for the year ahead.

Questions to Think About

1. What are your plans after high school? Will you go to college? To work?

2. Why do you think you will be successful?

Your Thoughts

_____

_____

_____

_____

_____

_____

_____

_____

_____

_____

PERSONAL DEVELOPMENT CHECKLIST

Student _____ **School Counselor** _____

Address each task as it becomes appropriate for your grade level. Check off tasks as they are completed, keeping in mind that not all tasks apply to all grades and that you may want to repeat some tasks. Your school counselor will be helpful in guiding you through this process.

Grades 6-12

Developed personal Success Team	6__ 7__ 8__ 9__ 10__ 11__ 12__
Took an interest inventory	6__ 7__ 8__ 9__ 10__ 11__ 12__
Explored resources in career center	6__ 7__ 8__ 9__ 10__ 11__ 12__
Used Internet to explore careers	6__ 7__ 8__ 9__ 10__ 11__ 12__
Identified appropriate career cluster	6__ 7__ 8__ 9__ 10__ 11__ 12__
Talked to adults about career plans	6__ 7__ 8__ 9__ 10__ 11__ 12__
Mentored another student	6__ 7__ 8__ 9__ 10__ 11__ 12__
Participated in school activities	6__ 7__ 8__ 9__ 10__ 11__ 12__
Volunteered in community activities	6__ 7__ 8__ 9__ 10__ 11__ 12__
Held leadership positions	6__ 7__ 8__ 9__ 10__ 11__ 12__
Took a career-related field trip	6__ 7__ 8__ 9__ 10__ 11__ 12__
Attended employer presentations	6__ 7__ 8__ 9__ 10__ 11__ 12__
Participated in a career day	6__ 7__ 8__ 9__ 10__ 11__ 12__
Listened to career speakers	6__ 7__ 8__ 9__ 10__ 11__ 12__
Talked to college representatives	6__ 7__ 8__ 9__ 10__ 11__ 12__
Spoke with employee in field of interest	6__ 7__ 8__ 9__ 10__ 11__ 12__
Observed or shadowed an employee	6__ 7__ 8__ 9__ 10__ 11__ 12__
Filled out a sample job application	6__ 7__ 8__ 9__ 10__ 11__ 12__
Completed a real job application	6__ 7__ 8__ 9__ 10__ 11__ 12__
Learned about and completed résumé	6__ 7__ 8__ 9__ 10__ 11__ 12__
Requested recommendation letters	6__ 7__ 8__ 9__ 10__ 11__ 12__
Participated in a practice interview	6__ 7__ 8__ 9__ 10__ 11__ 12__
Interviewed for a real job	6__ 7__ 8__ 9__ 10__ 11__ 12__
Held part-time or summer job	6__ 7__ 8__ 9__ 10__ 11__ 12__

Your Thoughts

_____
_____
_____
_____
_____
_____
_____
_____
_____
_____
_____

Things You Need to Do

_____
_____
_____
_____
_____
_____
_____
_____
_____
_____
_____
_____

BAD DECISIONS, BAD RESULTS

We are not born knowing how to make decisions, but we are expected to know how and that just does not make sense. If we are going to make decisions the right way, then we need to be taught a process. We need to learn and practice just like we do other skills, such as spelling and math, or playing an instrument. Those skills are taught in school, but unfortunately, decision making is not. Later in this book, we will show you a six-step process that will help you with any decision you ever have to make.

Good Decisions

A decision is good only if it is the right decision for the person who must live with the outcomes. People who talk about being satisfied with a decision or having it turn out the way they wanted took the process seriously and worked through it completely. Learn to make responsible, thoughtful decisions that will lead to choices that are best for you.

🔆 Questions to Think About

1. What kind of decision maker are you?

2. Were you ever taught how to make a decision?

3. What kind of process do you use when you are making important decisions?

✐ Your Thoughts

_____

_____

_____

_____

_____

_____

_____

WHAT KIND OF LIFE?

Ask an older person—a grandparent, uncle, family friend, neighbor—"What kind of life have you had?" and listen carefully to the answer. Is the answer "I have had a great life," or "I have not had a very good life at all"? What would you want your answer to be? Most of us want a satisfying life and one that is full of good things. So how can you make that happen?

Look Back at the Decisions You Have Made

In high school, you might look back on the ideas you had about work and education when you were in middle school and realize how much your thoughts have changed. Maybe courses you have taken, people you have met, or interests you have acquired have taken your career goals in new and different directions.

At the end of each chapter in this book, there are questions to help you understand what you have read and create personal meaning from it. It is important that you answer the questions honestly. You might want to look back at how you answered the questions when you were in middle school. How has your thinking changed and what have you learned about yourself?

Keep a Journal

You might want to keep a personal journal of the thoughts you have at the end of each chapter. Update your responses as your needs, wants, interests, values, and abilities change. This will give you an idea of how you feel about the key areas of your life and how those feelings may affect the decisions you have yet to make.

Are you happy with your life?

What kind of life do you want to have right now? Is there anything you wish you could change? Although change is not always easy, it might be worthwhile if you want to be happier with your life. Remember that choosing not to make a change is also a decision. Do you want to settle for the way things are or do something to make your life better?

💡 Questions to Think About

1. How do you feel about your life right now?

2. What would you change about it if you could?

3. What decisions could you make now so that your life will be better in the future?

💬 Your Thoughts

_____
_____
_____
_____
_____
_____
_____
_____
_____
_____

✏️ Things You Need to Do

_____
_____
_____
_____
_____
_____
_____
_____
_____

MAKE YOUR OWN DECISIONS

Ask adults to tell you about their lives and chances are they will talk about parts of their lives that did not turn out as expected. These may have been jobs, relationships, relocations, or maybe choices of college or career. Were they unhappy with decisions they made? Did they let others make decisions for them? Do they wish they could make some decisions over again? What would they do differently in order to get different results?

A Better Life

The more good decisions you make, the greater the probability that your life will be acceptable to you. The opposite holds true as well. If you continuously make poor choices, you are more likely to end up with a life that is neither as satisfying nor as acceptable as you want it to be.

As a teen, this is the time to learn, practice, and improve your decision-making skills. You will be better prepared to make important decisions the right way—carefully, thoughtfully, and deliberately. Decision making is not difficult, and the process itself is not complicated. Utilize the process described later in this book and take control of your life. The person who will benefit the most is you.

A Lifelong Skill

Learn and practice your decision-making skills and you will be better prepared to make the many significant life decisions that lie ahead. Decision making affects all areas of your life, and once you learn the process, you will use it again and again.

Determine What Is Best for You

Individuals who learn the decision-making process can still have difficulty making decisions because they do not make decisions and choices without involving and affecting other people in their lives. Family and friends offer opinions and influence our decisions. Parents and teachers ask us to explain and defend the choices we make. Their reactions can affect how confident we feel when we need to make future decisions. We may second-guess ourselves. With practice and commitment on your part, the decision-making process described in the chapters that follow will give you the confidence you need to move forward with your decisions.

When to Compromise

The influence of others is not the only factor that can affect our ability to make good decisions. Circumstances can, too. Sometimes, events beyond our control make it impossible for us to act on our first choices, forcing us to make decisions based on compromise. For example, you might decide not to participate in a sport because your family needs you to work. You might turn down a scholarship at an out-of-state college because you are afraid of the impact that decision might have on a relationship. Needing to care for a young sibling or an ailing parent might limit your college options.

Circumstances can limit your options and choices. When this happens, take the time to reevaluate and reprioritize your needs and wants in light of the new circumstances. Rethink the information you have gathered and then move through the decision-making process again until you are comfortable with another alternative.

💡 Questions to Think About

1. What can you learn about decision making from others?

2. When might the opinions of others be helpful?

3. Describe a compromise you made recently.

4. Why did you compromise?

5. What was the outcome of that decision?

6. Would you make the same decision again or a different one?

Your Thoughts

_____

_____

_____

_____

_____

_____

_____

_____

_____

_____

_____

SUCCESS TEAMS
AND SUCCESS PLANS

Do you play basketball or another team sport? If so, do you think you can win a game all by yourself? If you do not play a sport, have you been in a school play or are you a member of the band or chorus? Can you perform every role in the school play or entertain at halftime all alone? There are few, if any, times in life when success can be achieved by one person all alone. Teams have coaches to help players improve, and the players support each other to win games.

This kind of team success happens not only on the playing field but also in life. For you to succeed in school and in life, you need to be part of a team that will provide you with the assistance and support you need to overcome obstacles, academic or personal, that may stand in the way of reaching your academic and career goals.

Know When You Need Help

As soon as you identify obstacles, decide if you can overcome them on your own. If not, get the help you need. Asking for help is not a sign of weakness. It is actually a sign of maturity and shows others that you want to succeed, you are serious, and you are willing to do what is necessary to improve your life. Let others help you. Remember that few, if any, of us succeed alone.

Develop a Success Team and Success Plan

If you want to reach your academic and career goals, think about creating a personal Success Team and a Success Plan. There are people in your school and your community who care about you and want to help you succeed. Invite individuals to join your team who will support and assist you as you identify and overcome personal and academic issues that might stand in your way. Develop these relationships, and be sure to take advantage of support services available to you.

Now, using the Success Team Inventory and the Student Success Planner for your grade level, begin to assemble your Success Team and collect the information that will help you make the important academic and career decisions that lie ahead.

SUCCESS TEAM INVENTORY

Student _____ Primary Success Advisor _____

I. DETERMINING EDUCATIONAL AND VOCATIONAL GOALS

____ Complete interest survey
____ Clarify educational and career goals
____ Determine needs for further education

Team Members:

II. ACADEMIC ISSUES

Select areas in which you may need assistance.

____ Academic advisement	____ Study skills
____ Time management	____ Language barrier
____ Reading	____ Test anxiety
____ Course selection	____ Math anxiety
____ Degree requirements	____ Job readiness
____ Class attendance	____ Interview preparation
____ Writing skills	____ Résumé preparation
____ Grades	____ Job application
____ Tutoring	Other: _____

Team Members:

III. EXTRACURRICULAR ACTIVITIES

Select activities in which you may have an interest.

____ Athletics	____ Volunteer organizations
____ Performing arts	____ Clubs
____ Student government	Other: _____

Team Members:

IV. OVERCOMING POTENTIAL OBSTACLES

Identify obstacles to achieving your educational or vocational goals.

___ Financial   ___ Transportation
___ Relationships   ___ Employment
___ Housing   ___ Child care
Other: _____

Team Members:

V. HEALTH AND WELLNESS

Consider any health and wellness concerns you may want to address.

___ Drug use   ___ Alcohol abuse
___ Eating disorders   ___ Weight concerns
___ Pregnancy   ___ Physical concerns
___ Visual/hearing concerns   ___ Lack of exercise
___ Depression   Other: _____

Team Members:

VI. PERSONAL CIRCUMSTANCES

Consider any personal or family concerns that might interfere with your ability to succeed in school.

___ Unemployed family member   ___ Lack of family support
___ Parental separation or divorce   ___ Family member in jail
Other: _____

Team Members:

Action Steps and Timelines

_____

_____

_____

_____

_____

🔆 Questions to Think About

1. Are there certain teachers or other adults you go to with problems or questions?

2. Who could help you make career decisions?

3. Who could help you make educational decisions?

4. What might keep you from reaching your goals?

5. Who do you know who could help you overcome these obstacles?

6. Who will you ask to be on your Success Team?

💭 Your Thoughts

_____

_____

_____

_____

_____

_____

_____

_____

_____

_____

✏️ Things You Need to Do

_____

_____

_____

_____

_____

_____

_____

_____

_____

STUDENT SUCCESS PLANNER: MIDDLE SCHOOL

"What are you going to be when you grow up?" becomes a common question when you get into middle school. It is not too early to make some decisions that will influence your educational and career choices. The following topics will help you to identify your strengths, interests and aptitudes. Then you can begin to put together an educational plan that will help you reach your goals.

Personality Traits

Describe yourself.

_____

_____

_____

_____

_____

List three personal characteristics that would make you more successful in school.

_____

_____

_____

_____

_____

How do your grades in school affect how you feel about yourself?

_____

_____

_____

_____

_____

What qualities would make you more successful in school?

_____

_____

_____

_____

_____

Obstacles to Success

What issues or situations are affecting your behavior or your ability to do well in school?

_____

_____

_____

_____

_____

What problems at home or in school could you use help with?

_____

_____

_____

_____

_____

Values and Goals

Why is it important to do well in school?

_____

_____

_____

_____

_____

What plans do you have for your education and future career?

_____

_____

_____

_____

_____

Communication and Interpersonal Skills

How are your communication skills? Do you write well? Speak well?

_____

_____

_____

_____

_____

In what ways do you interact with others at school? How do you show people that you respect and appreciate diversity?

_____

_____

_____

_____

_____

Describe your behavior in school.

_____

_____

_____

_____

_____

Do you behave appropriately? Give an example of a time when you accepted responsibility for your actions.

_____

_____

_____

_____

_____

Interests and Hobbies

What school or community activities do you participate in?

_____

_____

_____

_____

_____

What hobbies and activities do you enjoy in your leisure time?

_____

_____

_____

_____

_____

Do you have any special interests?

_____

_____

_____

_____

_____

List a few things that you are particularly good at.

_____

_____

_____

_____

_____

Job Skills

What special skills or abilities do you have?

_____

_____

_____

_____

_____

Accomplishments

List a few accomplishments, projects, or activities that you are proud of.

_____

_____

_____

_____

_____

Aptitudes and Learning Styles

What are your favorite subjects at school? Why do you like them?

_____

_____

_____

_____

_____

What subjects do you get the best grades in? Why do you do well in them?

_____

_____

_____

_____

_____

How do you take responsibility for your learning? Is it your job to learn?

_____

_____

_____

_____

_____

Describe your study habits.

_____

_____

_____

_____

_____

Have you taken a learning style assessment? If so, what is your learning style?

_____

_____

_____

_____

_____

Are you doing well enough in school to reach your goals?

_____

_____

_____

_____

_____

If not, how do you plan to do better in school?

_____

_____

_____

_____

Plans after High School

___ Work   ___ Military: Branch _____

___ Two-year college   ___ Job training/apprenticeship

___ Four-year college ___ Trade/vocational school

Other: _____

Career Exploration

What is your definition of a career?

_____

_____

_____

_____

_____

What careers are you considering? What career cluster do you prefer?

_____

_____

_____

_____

What school subjects are important in those careers?

_____

_____

_____

_____

What careers *do not* interest you? Why not?

_____

_____

_____

_____

_____

Results of Career Assessment

Name of Assessment	Date	Results

Developmental Activities and Tasks

____ Added members to Success Team

____ Participated in school activities

____ Volunteered in community activities

____ Researched careers

____ Held leadership positions

____ Talked to parents/adults about career plan

____ Held part-time or summer job

____ Took an interest inventory

____ Participated in a career day

____ Took a career-related field trip

____ Observed/shadowed employee

____ Listened to career speakers

✎ Things You Need to Do

_____

_____

_____

_____

_____

_____

_____

_____

_____

STUDENT SUCCESS PLANNER: HIGH SCHOOL

Use this planner to collect information about yourself. Then, when you need to make personal, educational, and career decisions, you will be ready. Be sure to update the information every school year because your interests and abilities may change.

Personality Traits

These traits are desirable in higher education and in the workplace. Which of your experiences would demonstrate that you have these traits?

Responsibility:

_____
_____
_____

Self-esteem:

_____
_____
_____

Sociability:

_____
_____
_____

Integrity/Honesty:

_____
_____
_____

Cooperation:

_____
_____
_____

Values and Goals

Why is it important to do well in school?

_____

_____

_____

_____

_____

What is important to you in a career?

_____

_____

_____

_____

_____

Obstacles to Success

What issues or situations are affecting your behavior or your ability to do well in school?

_____

_____

_____

_____

_____

What problems at home or in school could you use help with?

_____

_____

_____

_____

_____

Communication and Interpersonal Skills

How are your communication skills? Do you write well? Speak well?

_____

_____

_____

_____

_____

In what ways do you interact with others at school? At work? How do you show people that you respect and appreciate diversity?

_____
_____
_____
_____
_____

Describe your behavior in school.

_____
_____
_____
_____
_____

Do you behave appropriately? Give an example of a time when you accepted responsibility for your actions.

_____
_____
_____
_____
_____

Interests and Hobbies

What school or community activities do you participate in?

_____
_____
_____
_____

What hobbies and activities do you enjoy in your leisure time?

_____
_____
_____
_____

Do you have any special interests?

_____

_____

_____

_____

_____

List a few things that you are particularly good at.

_____

_____

_____

_____

_____

Job Skills

What skills or abilities do you have that might interest an employer?

_____

_____

_____

_____

_____

Accomplishments

List a few accomplishments, projects, or activities that you are proud of.

_____

_____

_____

_____

_____

Aptitudes and Learning Styles

What are your favorite school subjects? Why do you like them best?

_____

_____

_____

_____

_____

What subjects do you get the best grades in? Why do you do well in them?

_____

_____

_____

_____

_____

How do you take responsibility for your learning? Is it your job to learn?

_____

_____

_____

_____

_____

Describe your study habits.

_____

_____

_____

_____

_____

Have you taken a learning style assessment? If so, what is your learning style?

_____

_____

_____

_____

_____

Are you doing well enough in school to reach your educational and career goals?

_____

_____

_____

_____

_____

If not, how do you plan to do better in school?

_____

_____

_____

_____

_____

Plans after High School

___ Work   ___ Military: Branch _____

___ Two-year college   ___ Job training/apprenticeship

___ Four-year college   ___ Trade/vocational school

Other: _____

Career Exploration

What kinds of things are important to you in a career?

_____

_____

_____

_____

_____

What career cluster do you prefer? What careers are you considering?

_____

_____

_____

_____

_____

What school subjects are important in those careers?

_____

_____

_____

_____

_____

Results of Career Assessment

Name of Assessment	Date	Results

Developmental Activities and Tasks

___ Added members to Success Team

___ Participated in school activities

___ Volunteered in community activities

___ Researched careers

___ Held leadership positions

___ Requested recommendation letters

___ Attended a college fair

___ Completed job applications

___ Mentored other students

___ Talked to parents/adults about career plan

___ Held part-time or summer job

___ Took an interest inventory

___ Observed/shadowed employee

___ Took a career-related field trip

___ Participated in a career day

___ Had a practice interview

___ Interviewed an employee

___ Completed college applications

___ Participated in job interview

___ Listened to career speakers

Work Experience (Include Volunteer Experiences)

Employer	Dates	Type of Work	Skills

Important Documentation

    ____ Transcript of grades

    ____ Employment credentials: skill competencies or certificates

    ____ Completed résumé

    ____ Copies of completed job and/or college applications

    ____ Special achievement awards

    ____ List of references

Standardized Test Scores

HSPA _____

PSAT/NMSQT _____

ACT _____ ACT _____ SAT _____ SAT _____

ASVAB _____

Competency exam _____

Other: _____

✎ Things You Need to Do

_____

_____

_____

_____

_____

_____

_____

_____

_____

_____

MAKING DECISIONS IN LIFE'S SEVEN BIG-TICKET AREAS

To understand the role that decision making plays in your life, consider the areas that have the greatest impact on the quality of a person's life. As a teenager, it is important that you start becoming familiar with what can be called life's big-ticket decisions.

Throughout your life, you will make decisions in seven big-ticket areas and the choices that you make along the way will define the quality of your life and the direction it will take. The decisions that matter most are the ones you make from now on.

Become an effective decision maker, gain greater control of your life, and find more satisfaction in the choices you make. Accept responsibility for the decisions you make. Commit to deliberate and thoughtful decision making. Learn, practice, and apply the six-step process below. (This process will be explained in greater detail in a later chapter.) You will have greater confidence in the decisions you make and you will realize greater academic, career, and personal success in your life.

What is the six-step decision-making process?

1. Define the decision to be made.
2. Evaluate your needs and wants.
3. Compile a list of realistic alternatives.
4. Investigate each alternative.
5. Determine the best alternative.
6. Establish a plan and implement it.

Evaluate Your Life as It Is Now

If you want to create a more fulfilling life, begin by evaluating your life as it is now. Consider, now and throughout your life, whether you need to change certain aspects of your life. Think specifically about the seven big-ticket areas.

Education	Field of study/major
Career choice	Relationships/friends
Health and wellness	Leisure activities
Environment (living and working)	

People who make good decisions in all seven big-ticket areas are more likely to be satisfied with the lives they have. For example, the initial decisions you make regarding your education and field of study will play a big part in the career you choose, which will affect your living and work environments, the relationships you develop, your health and wellness, and how much leisure time you will have. How satisfied you are in each area will determine how you feel about the life you create for yourself.

Using the decision-making process to organize relevant information and define alternatives will increase your chances of choosing the one that will be best for you. Make good decisions in all seven of the big-ticket areas of your life and chances are, when you are asked, "What kind of life have you had?" you will be able to answer, "I have had a *great* life!"

⋰⃝ Questions to Think About

1. Which big-ticket areas are most important to you now? Why?

2. How would you describe your life over this past year in the big-ticket areas?

3. Choose three big-ticket areas in which you have made decisions recently. How did your decisions turn out?

4. Is there anything that you would do differently to change the results?

⌾ Your Thoughts

_____

_____

_____

_____

_____

Education

Students who understand the importance of education and the roles it can play in their lives are much more likely to be successful in school. Part of figuring that out is giving some thought to what you might want to do when you are an adult. What careers or occupations interest you? What are you good at? How will you define success when you are an adult? By how much money you make? How happy you are? How much status, power, or prestige you have? How your work helps others or the environment? What education will be required? Will you need more than a high school education? Will you need additional vocational training or a college degree?

Whether you know exactly what you want to do or be is not as important as understanding that without education, your options will be limited. Education opens doors. Lack of education closes them. Through education, you acquire knowledge and skills that will be useful in work and in life. Keep your future in your sights. Set goals and then, once you have reached them, set new goals.

Questions to Think About

1. Ask individuals who did not finish high school about their decisions to drop out. How do they feel about those decisions now?

2. What do you want to do after you graduate from high school?

3. What jobs or careers are you considering?

4. How much education do those careers require?

5. How will you choose the career(s) that would be right for you?

6. What resources and what people can help you make these decisions?

Your Thoughts

_____

_____

_____

_____

_____

_____

_____

_____

Field of Study

Why choose a field of study? Why not just leave your options completely open? As we mature and experience life, we learn more about ourselves. We identify our strengths and weaknesses. We learn what interests us, and, just as importantly, what we do not want to do. That self-knowledge is critical information when choosing an occupation or career.

Occupational clusters can help you with your career exploration and your research will clarify, among other things, what education will be required. Then, as you move through school, you will want to choose courses and a major that will lead to occupations that will allow you to be successful and satisfied. Remember, too, that education is necessary not only to get a job but also to keep a job and to get a better one. If we are to keep up with advances in technology and developments in the workplace, we need to accept personal responsibility for lifelong learning.

Questions to Think About

1. How will you choose a field of study?

2. What field of study is most appealing to you at this point in time?

3. What jobs or careers will that field of study prepare you for?

Your Thoughts

_____
_____
_____
_____
_____
_____

Career Choice

Begin the process of identifying possible careers by gathering two types of information. The first is information about yourself, which you can get through self-assessment. The insight you gain from self-assessment will help you identify career alternatives and work environments that are in line with your interests, skills, and values. Self-assessment instruments are useful as you compile and organize this data.

Interest inventories, for example, are developed from the personality theory that people who share similar likes and dislikes usually enjoy performing similar types of work in similar environments. Interest inventory results will help you to narrow down which careers might be right for you. Ask your counselor what self-assessment resources (e.g. Self-Directed Search, Strong Interest Inventory) are available through your school or on the Internet.

Next, you will want to gather information about careers that are compatible with your self-assessment data. Although there are thousands of occupations, focus your research on careers that people with your personality traits are most likely to choose. Using occupational clusters will allow you to be more efficient in your research because you will identify only those careers that most closely match who you are. You simply find the cluster of occupations that best matches your interests. After you have identified the cluster that seems to be the most suitable for you, you will be ready to start your career research.

It is important that you do sufficient research and identify as many possible careers as you can. Unfortunately, people often limit their research to the few careers they know about and ignore many other possibilities. At some point you will want to consider additional issues, such as lifestyles that different careers offer and the current and future demand for these careers. For now, research occupations for which your self-assessment data indicate you would be well suited.

Questions to Think About

1. How would you describe yourself?

2. What are your interests? What are your abilities?

3. What career research have you done so far?

4. Why are both self-assessment and career research important in making a career choice?

Your Thoughts

_____

_____

_____

_____

_____

Living and Work Environments

How we feel about where we live and work can have a significant bearing on how satisfied we are with our lives. Your living environment incorporates what part of the country you live in, your community and neighborhood, your apartment or house, and whether you live in the city or in the country. How do you feel about where you live? Are there things that you wish you could change?

Our work environments—whether for part-time jobs or career positions—also impact our satisfaction with our lives. What is important to you in a work environment? Would you prefer working indoors or outdoors? Would you rather move around or be stationary? Which is more appealing—a small, medium, or large company? Would you be more comfortable in a casual atmosphere or one that is more professional? Every job has a corresponding environment; your objective is to find a job you like in a place you want to spend your time. People who fail to consider their work environments will likely be unhappy even if they are working in occupations they enjoy.

Questions to Think About

1. How do you feel about your living environment?

2. What would you change about it if you could?

3. If you have held a job, describe your work environment.

4. What did you like and dislike about that work environment?

5. If you have not ever held a job, what do you think will be important to you in your work environment?

Your Thoughts

_____

_____

_____

_____

_____

Relationships

Unless you live alone on an island, you most likely interact with and develop relationships with a number of other people. The quality of these relationships can play an important role in determining how satisfied you are with your life. When you are unhappy or unsatisfied with your life, you may overlook the part that relationships can play in that discontent. These relationships can influence your life in both positive and negative ways. Because of the significant roles that others play in your life, it is important that you approach decisions about relationships in the same way you do other big-ticket decisions.

Questions to Think About

1. Who are the most significant people in your life?

2. Who are your role models? Why are they important to you?

3. How do your relationships with your peers make you feel?

4. Describe a time when a friend influenced your decision in a way that was good for him or her but not necessarily good for you?

5. Who do you turn to for help making important decisions?

6. Have you ever gone against the opinion of one of these people when making a decision? How did the decision turn out?

7. Who would you trust to help you plan your future?

Your Thoughts

_____

_____

_____

_____

_____

Health and Wellness

Your physical health and wellness, in addition to your intellectual, social, and spiritual well-being, significantly influence how you feel about your life. Assessing any and all of your health and wellness issues and making the right decisions in these areas will improve your attitude toward the other big-ticket areas of your life.

Are you dissatisfied with how you look or how you feel? Does your self-esteem suffer because of it? Is your attitude or your behavior in other areas of your life affected? Do you smoke, drink alcohol, or abuse medications? Is your weight what it should be? Do you eat healthy foods? Do you exercise?

Take time to evaluate your personal habits, schedule a yearly physical, and address existing conditions. Assess your personal wellness behaviors. Adopt a healthier lifestyle. Take control of your personal health and wellness by making thoughtful decisions and well-informed choices.

Questions to Think About

1. How do your health and wellness affect how satisfied you are with your life?

2. What decisions have you made that have affected your health and wellness in a positive way?

3. What decisions have affected your health and wellness in a negative way?

Your Thoughts

_____

_____

_____

_____

_____

Leisure Activities

A satisfying life is one that is balanced, and leisure can bring that balance to our lives. Do you schedule time for leisure activities in your daily or weekly routine? Do you decide how you want to spend your free time, or do you simply let it happen without structure or routine? Do you think of school as a boring place? Is school really boring, or is it you? Is your decision *not* to get involved in school activities the cause of your boredom?

Being active in school and the community is a great way to connect with students who have interests in common with you. Extracurricular activities like chorus, orchestra, special-interest clubs and organizations, theater, student government, intramural or team sports can not only give you opportunities for success outside of the classroom, but also give you the chance to develop skills that will be valuable in the workplace later on. At the very least, group activities may bring personal enjoyment and give you the chance to relax and be yourself.

💡 Questions to Think About

1. What are your hobbies?

2. What special interests do you have?

3. Which community activities or organizations are you involved with?

4. What school clubs or activities do you participate in?

5. Which organizations or activities would you like to try?

6. How can being involved in clubs or organizations now, help you later?

Your Thoughts

_____
_____
_____
_____
_____
_____
_____
_____
_____
_____
_____

✏️ Things You Need to Do

_____
_____
_____
_____
_____
_____
_____
_____
_____
_____

An Effective Decision-Making Process

Decision Making Requires a Consistent Effort

If you are really committed to making the right choices and the best decisions for your life, then you must be willing to put forth genuine effort throughout the entire decision-making process. People who fail to make good decisions are often simply unwilling to commit to the entire process which limited their chances of achieving favorable results.

Some who lack commitment would rather let others make their choices for them. They shift responsibility for their decisions to someone else and then complain when they are unhappy with the results. Accepting responsibility for making your own decisions is important. Learning how to effectively utilize the six steps in this decision-making process will help you make decisions properly and increase your chances for positive outcomes.

Six Steps in Decision Making

Decision making is not difficult, yet people often feel confused or overwhelmed when they face major decisions. Many lack the information they need to make good decisions because they skip over or ignore important parts of the process. By completing each step, they increase the likelihood that their choices will reflect the alternatives that best meet their most important needs and wants.

Simple, everyday decisions are made somewhat automatically. However, when a more complex decision needs to be made, it is important to work through the following steps:

Step 1: **D**efine the decision to be made.

Step 2: **E**valuate your most important needs and wants.

Step 3: **C**ompile a list of realistic alternatives.

Step 4: **I**nvestigate each alternative.

Step 5: **D**etermine the best alternative.

Step 6: **E**stablish a plan and implement it.

D-E-C-I-D-E

It is imperative that you address each component of the process if you want to be satisfied with the outcome. Many people are dissatisfied with their lives because, when faced with important decisions, they overlook the importance of addressing all of the steps in the process, and as a result, they have difficulty choosing the best alternative.

Those who are the most dissatisfied usually jump from Step 2, identifying their needs and wants, to Step 5, choosing an alternative. They fail to gather the information they need about their alternatives in order to select the best options. When intermediate steps are skipped, the decision maker is unable to determine which alternative is best.

Step 1. Define the decision to be made.

The first step in the decision-making process is to recognize the need to make a decision. Which college will you attend? What will your major be? Do you want to find a better job? Are you unhappy with a significant relationship? Are you considering changing schools? Even if the decision you have to make is a complex one, you need to be able to write it down. How would you state it to someone else? This may seem overly simple, but it is where you need to begin.

Step 2. Evaluate your most important needs and wants.

In order to select the best option for you, you will need to put a personal filtering system in place. This is basically all of the information that you will use as criteria to rank your alternatives. Make a list of needs and wants that are most important to you. Then, identify the top ten that you will use to filter and rank your alternatives in anticipation of making your final decision. Two charts follow that will help you visualize this part of the process.

SAMPLE JOB DECISION CHART

Needs/Wants	Choice A	Choice B	Choice C	Choice D
1. Salary	X		X	
2. Work Environment	X		X	X
3. Pleasant People		X	X	X
4. Work Activities	X		X	X
5. Challenges/Problems		X	X	X
6. Weekend Hours	X	X	X	
7. Psychological Rewards		X		X
8. Job Security	X		X	X
9. Close to Home	X	X	X	
10. Flexible Schedule			X	X
	60%	50%	90%	70%

SAMPLE COLLEGE DECISION CHART

Needs/Wants	Choice A	Choice B	Choice C	Choice D
1. Curriculum	X	X		X
2. Location/Environment	X		X	X
3. Quality of Academics	X	X	X	
4. Cost ($5,000-$15,000)	X		X	X
5. Financial Aid (Scholarships)		X	X	
6. Size (7,500-12,000)	X	X	X	X
7. Class Size (<35)	X		X	
8. Co-op/Internships	X			X
9. Facilities	X	X		X
10. Recreation/Clubs	X		X	
	90%	50%	70%	60%

DECISION-MAKING CHART

Decision: _____

Most Important Criteria		**Alternatives**		
(Needs/Wants)	Choice A	Choice B	Choice C	Choice D
1.				
2.				
3.				
4.				
5.				
6.				
7.				
8.				
9.				
10.				
	___%	___%	___%	___%

Best alternative: _____

Second best: _____

Third best: _____

Fourth best: _____

Step 3. Compile a list of realistic alternatives.

Gathering self-assessment information is a critical component of the decision-making process; however, you will also need to gather information about the topic of your decision so that you can identify all possible, realistic options. You will need to do sufficient research to feel confident that you have identified the alternatives that satisfy your most important needs and wants. You will have an opportunity to expand your possibilities beyond those that are obvious and discover others that may never have come to mind. It is not unusual for this part of the process to feel overwhelming. Just remember that your goal is to expand your alternatives beyond the one or two that you already knew about.

Step 4. Investigate each alternative to gather necessary information.

After you have identified viable alternatives, you will need to gather additional information specific to each alternative. During this important phase of the decision-making process, you will analyze each alternative carefully and consider the pros and cons for each possibility based on your most important needs and wants, which you identified in Step 2. This will help you identify the best alternative.

Remember, you will not be able to identify which is the best choice for you unless you know what criteria you are trying to satisfy. The criteria that you identified were incorporated into your personal filtering system and will help you select the best alternative.

Step 5. Determine the best alternative.

After you have gathered information on each alternative, choose the one that you feel satisfies the criteria most important to you by determining which of the alternatives satisfies your most significant needs and wants. The alternative you choose will be the one that offers you the greatest chance of experiencing a favorable outcome.

As you may have guessed, it is possible that none of the alternatives will meet all of your most important needs and wants. You should, though, be able to identify the alternative that satisfies the highest percentage of your criteria. The option that meets 85 or 90 percent of what you need to feel satisfied will outrank those that meet only 50, 60, or 70 percent of your wants and needs. Your goal is to identify the best alternative from among those you have researched and to meet most, if not all, of your criteria for that particular decision.

Step 6. Establish a plan and implement it.

Developing a plan of action is the most important step in any decision. It is that point in time when a decision maker chooses the best alternative and accepts responsibility for the decision. Many people complete Steps 1 through 5, but then they choose not to act on their decisions. They may be overwhelmed, fearful, or unable to bring the process to an end. Others may simply be unwilling to give themselves permission to act on their decisions.

Be mindful of the fact that not making a decision is, in itself, a choice. By choosing to do nothing, you have decided that accepting the status quo is your best alternative. Are you unwilling to change? Are you afraid to move into a new situation? Is doing nothing an acceptable option? If not, work to overcome whatever stands in your way. Those who complete all the steps of the decision-making process move forward with confidence and are able to establish a plan of action that includes goals and timelines for implementing their decisions.

If the outcome of a decision is different than what you expected, a simple modification may give you the results you hoped for. New information may come to your attention and give you reason to change your initial decision or adjust your plan. That is not only acceptable, but advisable. Making adjustments, even after you have begun to implement your plan, will often make a good plan better.

☼ Questions to Think About

1. When have you used the six-step decision-making process to make one or more big-ticket decisions?

2. How well did the process work for you?

3. Which step was most difficult for you? Which was most helpful?

4. Did you want to skip certain steps of the process? Which ones and why?

5. What actions did you take to implement your decisions?

Your Thoughts

_____

_____

_____

_____

_____

_____

_____

_____

_____

_____

Things You Need to Do

_____

_____

_____

_____

_____

_____

_____

_____

_____

_____

_____

RIGHT EXIT, RIGHT STREET

The concept of occupational clusters is not always easy to understand. One way of visualizing clusters is to imagine that you are driving in a car on a major roadway that has multiple exits. Each exit represents a different occupational cluster. For example, Exit 1 could be Business, Exit 2 Health, Exit 3 Engineering, Exit 4 Education, Exit 5 Computers, and so on. In the early stages of your career exploration, you will want to get off at the exit that is the most appealing to you.

After you have chosen an exit, you will want to focus on a particular occupation within your chosen cluster. To do this, think of the exit as taking you into a neighborhood. As you drive through the neighborhood, the streets you pass represent specific occupations within the broader cluster. For example, if you take the business exit into the business neighborhood, you might come upon streets named Accounting Avenue, Management Plaza, Real Estate Road, Insurance Lane, Entrepreneurship Way, Human Resources Street, Sales and Marketing Place, Economics Square, and Finance Circle. Find the street that best represents the environment in which you will feel most comfortable. The street may also give you an indication of which field of study you might want to pursue.

When choosing your street, think back to the interests, skills, and values that you want to be able to express in the workplace. Finding the right occupation means finding an environment that will allow you the opportunity for self-expression and a job that will let you make the best use of your talents. Your goal is to get paid for doing something you enjoy in an environment you feel comfortable in, while working with people who have interests similar to yours.

Right Street, Right House

Finding the right exit and the right street are important, but you still need to consider which house on that street you will want to live in, which will represent your best fit in the working world. The people who live in that house are those who you will be able to relate to the most. Let's say you get off the Education exit and turn on to Teacher Avenue. Your interests may be in working with young children, so you will choose the house where elementary school teachers live rather than the houses where high school teachers or college professors live. A major in elementary education then becomes a logical academic choice for your field of study.

The concept of highway, exit, street, and house will help you visualize the environments in which you will be able to express your interests, skills, and values. It offers a simple way to understand more clearly what you need to do in order to identify academic and career choices that will be right for you.

Right Occupation, Wrong Location

Sometimes people are in the right occupations but in the wrong places. In other words, they are not unhappy with their educational paths or careers but they are displeased with their current jobs. Some seek counseling or enroll in career development classes and, after some serious self-assessment and career exploration, they realize that they are simply not in the right place. If you think you are choosing the right career cluster, ask yourself, "Within that cluster, what would be the best environment for me to work in?" It is not enough just to identify an occupation or a particular job; it is equally important to find the right work environment.

If You Are Unhappy, Do Something to Change

You may have a part-time job that you do not like, but you are choosing to stay. You are settling, accepting things as they are. Doing nothing to improve your current situation is a decision. When you decide to stay in an unsatisfying situation, you are deciding not to change. Your decision is intentional and deliberate. The consequences of staying where you are will most likely lead to growing feelings of dissatisfaction with the work component of your life. You owe it to yourself, and probably to your employer, to look for a new job.

💡 Questions to Think About

1. What interest tests can help you identify occupations you might like?

2. How can the highways/exits/neighborhoods/houses concept help you to choose an occupation or field of study?

3. Are there things about your life that you do not like? What are you doing to change them?

4. Have you ever avoided making a decision and regretted it? What was the situation and why did you have regrets?

Your Thoughts

_____
_____
_____
_____
_____
_____
_____
_____
_____
_____

Things You Need to Do

_____
_____
_____
_____
_____
_____
_____
_____
_____
_____
_____

DECIDING TO BE SUCCESSFUL IN SCHOOL

What decisions do you need to make in order to be a successful student? Make the most of your ability and achieve the highest level of education that you can. Knowledge not only makes you employable, but it will also help you to stay employed. Regardless of what educational path you take, you can be a more successful student if you choose to make four simple decisions.

Go and Participate

The first choice is the simplest one, but it is often the reason students fail in school. Make this your most important decision, as simple as it may sound. Go to school and go to class. You can't be successful if you don't show up! Being present physically is not enough though; you need to be present mentally. You need to pay attention and participate if you are going to learn. If your mind is not focused on what is being discussed in class, you are not learning. Be attentive. Learn something new in every class every day.

Get Help as Soon as You Know You Need It

The second decision successful students make is to get help as soon as they know they need it. When you first realize that a lesson or course is giving you problems, ask for help from your teacher, a friend, or a tutor. Take advantage of academic support services available at your school and in your community. You can overcome learning obstacles, but only you know when they need to be addressed.

Too many students simply do not get help when they need it. They believe or want to believe that they can do it on their own. Seeking assistance is not a sign of weakness. It is just the opposite. Smart students are the ones who know when they need help and get it. Try it and you will see how getting help can make you a better student.

Get Involved Outside of the Classroom

Your third decision is to get involved. Become an active participant in activities outside the classroom. You can develop useful life skills by participating in clubs and organizations while doing what you enjoy. To gain the maximum benefit, make an effort to make the club better. You will develop skills and become more confident. This will be important to you when you are asked to describe yourself in a job interview, because work environments are like clubs in many respects. An employer who learns that you were active and involved will assume that you will be like that at work as well. Through clubs and organizations, you gain experience, develop relationships, and acquire skills that are important in the workplace.

Finish What You Start

The fourth and final decision the successful student makes is to finish. Finish what you start. Finish your assignments, finish every course, finish the term, and finish your degree. Too many students drop out of school. They leave for a variety of reasons, good and bad, but no matter the reason, it is a fateful decision.

Talk to someone who dropped out of high school or someone who started college and quit before finishing. Their stories will give you all the motivation you will need to stay in school. Today's job market practically demands the completion of a high school diploma and, in many cases, a postsecondary degree or certificate. Determine what level of education you will need to be successful in your career of choice, and then don't stop until you obtain it.

If you are still not convinced of the value of education, try this experiment. Ask individuals you think are successful to tell you how they feel about education. Then ask the same question of people who are unemployed or work at jobs you think are unappealing, low paying, or unchallenging. Ask all of them what kind of students they were. If they were poor students or dropped out before completing high school, ask them if they wish they had stayed in school and tried harder. Would they approach education differently if given another chance?

What you choose to do in terms of education is one of the most significant life decisions you will make. Your decision will have a major impact on what kind of career and life you will have. How much of a commitment are you willing to make to your education?

⌄ Questions to Think About

1. Which four important decisions should you make in order to be successful in school?

2. Which of these decisions have you already made?

3. Are there obstacles that are keeping you from making the others?

4. What new decisions do you need to make?

5. Do you have any thoughts of not finishing high school? If so, have you talked to an adult about the consequences?

Your Thoughts

_____

_____

_____

_____

_____

_____

_____

_____

_____

_____

_____

✎ Things You Need to Do

_____

_____

_____

_____

_____

_____

_____

_____

_____

_____

DECISION MAKING
AND THE JOB SEARCH

If you are old enough to hold a part-time or summer job, the decision-making process can easily be applied to the job search. If you want to find a job that will take full advantage of your abilities and interests, begin by identifying your most important needs and wants. Then, in keeping with the process, you will identify, research, and select employment alternatives. Keep in mind that your success in landing a job will depend on how well you can communicate the value of your abilities and interests to prospective employers.

Analyze Potential Opportunities

To determine your potential value to an employer, begin by identifying and analyzing potential job opportunities. Every position has a job description that consists of simple phrases that summarize the activities, tasks, and roles that an individual must be able to perform to meet the job's requirements. Try to relate your skills and abilities to the functions of the jobs you want to pursue. Evaluate yourself honestly and completely.

Focus on Employer Needs and Challenges

An employer will want you to be able to fulfill specific needs of the organization. Employers identify problems, justify needs, and then fill positions. Your initial challenge is to determine just what it is that the employer needs the candidate to do for them. Once you have that figured out, you will be able to see yourself not as a person looking for a job, but as the answer to the employer's need. Then it is just a matter of communicating that to the employer. The more persuasive you can be, the sooner you will be employed.

The Greater the Need, the Better the Salary

Most people want to be paid what they believe they are worth. An employer must believe that you are competent and able to address the needs of the organization. If they see you as an asset and a solution to their problems, you just might earn what you are worth.

Inventory Your Past Experiences

Determine your value by analyzing your past experiences. Your most meaningful skills and abilities were probably acquired and fine-tuned through volunteering, jobs you have held, your classes, and school-related activities.

By thinking about what you have done, you will be able to inventory your skills. Once you know what you have to offer an employer, you need only to communicate your strengths clearly and confidently. By effectively identifying and then speaking about your skills, you will be able to demonstrate your value to an employer.

Fill Up an Imaginary Basket

To take stock of your past experiences, pretend that you are holding an imaginary basket in your arms. Now imagine that everything you have ever experienced is in that basket—every course you have taken, club you have been a part of, job you have had, team you have been on, and activity you have participated in.

Do not forget to put your accomplishments and achievements in your imaginary basket, too. Do not leave anything out, because the experiences in your basket tell your life story and represent your proudest moments.

Take the Best Out of Your Basket

Once your basket is full, begin to sort out the contents. Which skills are the strongest? Which experiences are the most significant? Which of your accomplishments would interest an employer? Which achievements demonstrate skills that are important in the workplace?

To impress an employer, you will identify specific skills and abilities that you have developed and explain how they will benefit the company. Have examples ready to prove that you can do what you say you can. The more convincing you are in describing how your skills match those required for a specific job, the better your chances of getting that job.

Are You a Ship with Anchors?

If your basket is not giving you confidence in your abilities, imagine instead that you are a ship—any kind of ship. A cruise ship, oil tanker, or aircraft carrier. Now imagine that you are traveling around the world, and along the way you pull into a port. Wanting to stay awhile, you drop anchor. As a job seeker or a student seeking a leadership position in school, you are a lot like a ship; instead of anchoring in different ports, you have been sailing from experience to experience, job to job, or activity to activity. You, too, have dropped anchors in the form of your strengths—the skills and abilities that you have used to get jobs done and done well. Just as a ship's anchor keeps it at port, your strengths will help keep you at a job or make you an effective student leader.

Think about it. Whenever you experienced success in the past, was it because others identified you as having the ability to do the job and sought you out when they needed your skills? Are you a writer for the school paper, a good speaker, computer whiz, a class or club officer, or an organizer? If someone asked you to list your strengths, what would you say? Which anchors will you talk about? What do you do best and how might your anchors relate to a position or job?

Prioritize Your Strengths

The next step is to prioritize your strengths. Prepare yourself to talk only about your higher order skills and your most significant accomplishments. For example, if you feel you have developed strong leadership skills by participating in school activities, talk about your most recent experience. Do not go back to an elementary school example if you have a more recent one to talk about. You want an interviewer to understand how you have developed skills that could transfer easily to the work environment.

Be Specific about Your Value

No matter what examples you use to promote your skills, stay focused on the group's or employer's needs. Limit your examples to the experiences where you met the needs of an organization or group. You will want to clearly communicate your value in terms of your abilities and knowledge.

Communicate Clearly What It Is You Want

Assess your past experiences and identify your strengths, and your confidence will surely grow. You will be able to demonstrate in a variety of ways why you are the most qualified individual to assume an important role. A focused and confident presentation will greatly increase your chances of success.

Prepare to Find Your Ideal Work Situation

For many people, work has a negative connotation: they dread going to work every day. You do not have to be one of them. Your goal should be to someday find work in a favorable environment where you can be productive, satisfied in your interactions with your coworkers, and gratified in your work. Accomplish that and you will have found your ideal work situation—you will be paid for doing something that you enjoy and do well.

Questions to Think About

1. Why is it important to consider your individual needs and wants when looking for a job?

2. What do abilities and interests have to do with occupational choice?

3. Why is it important to inventory past experiences?

4. Why will employers care about those experiences?

5. What experiences could you put into your basket to prove your skills?

6. What skills will be important for you to develop?

7. How would you describe your ideal work situation?

Your Thoughts

_____
_____
_____
_____
_____
_____
_____
_____
_____
_____
_____

Things You Need to Do

_____
_____
_____
_____
_____
_____
_____
_____
_____
_____

PERSONALITY, ABILITIES, AND CAREER CHOICE

An individual's personality can have a tremendous influence on whether he or she is a match for a particular career, occupation, or a specific job in a particular work environment. What kind of a person are you? How will your personality come into play in the workplace? Does your personality influence how you perform your job duties? How might personal traits and characteristics impact satisfaction with career and occupational choice?

Think of an office or a department within a company in the same way that you would a family; people hire others who they want in their work families. That is not surprising given that most of us will spend more hours at work than at home or anywhere else. Hiring managers evaluate job candidates not only on their skills, experience, and knowledge, but also on how well they think candidates will fit in. Compatibility, an often overlooked factor, is essential if the work environment is to be a positive one.

What Are Your Strongest Qualities?

Before you consider any career, occupation, or even a particular job, it is a good idea to ask yourself this question: What are the personal characteristics that an individual needs to possess in order to be successful in this field?

Do you need to be accurate, personable, flexible, focused, open-minded, outgoing, or persuasive? Next, list the adjectives that best describe you. Now compare what the job requires with your personal traits. The more matches, the better the fit.

Develop strong examples to support or prove why you are right for the position. This will give you confidence in your ability to do the job, and that attitude will come across in an interview. You will be prepared to explain just how your personality makes you the right candidate for the job.

How Do You Manage Yourself?

Getting a job is one thing; keeping it is something else entirely. In many cases, people are not fired for lack of knowledge or skills but because they did not or could not manage themselves properly. A bank teller who is habitually late to work will likely be let go even if he is conscientious in the performance of his duties. The salesperson that is rude or impatient with customers will certainly be fired even if she is the most knowledgeable about the store's merchandise. The lifeguard who texts and talks on his phone while on duty will be looking for a new job before the summer is over. Strong self-management skills are not only valuable; they are essential in school and in work. Teachers and employers will teach you the specifics of a subject or duties of a job, but they are less likely to teach you how to discipline and manage yourself.

How would you describe your work ethic? In other words, what kind of student or worker are you? Are you hardworking, conscientious, dependable, self-motivated, patient, cooperative, punctual, honest? Think of as many words as you can to describe yourself. What words would you use to describe your positive qualities? How about your not-so-positive qualities? Be honest. Work to improve your negative ways and habits. Accept the responsibility for managing your time and your behavior. Develop a work ethic you can be proud of.

Be Prepared with Evidence and Examples

Although it may be easy for you to select words from a list to describe yourself, you need to be able to provide examples to prove that you possess each of those particular characteristics. Preparation is the key. Do not underestimate the importance of being able to talk with confidence about your strengths and how they relate to particular school activities or part-time jobs. Those who have, and can prove they have, the strongest skills and most relevant qualities will be chosen to lead the club or be hired to do the work. They will also be the individuals most satisfied with their decisions.

Be Honest with Yourself

When making decisions, particularly those concerning careers and occupations, consider how the personality characteristics called for in various work environments may or may not reflect your own. Identify your personality traits and self-management style. Which occupational alternatives would best match your personality? An honest and thorough self-assessment is critical in the decision-making process if you expect to achieve favorable outcomes.

Questions to Think About

1. What does your personality have to do with your choice of career?

2. How could you find out what personality fits best with a specific occupation?

3. Which of your personal characteristics might interest employers?

4. What examples could you give to prove that you have specific traits, strengths, and characteristics?

Your Thoughts

_____
_____
_____
_____
_____
_____
_____
_____
_____
_____
_____

Things You Need to Do

_____
_____
_____
_____
_____
_____
_____
_____
_____

LIFE-CHANGING EVENTS

Most of us will experience one or more significant, life-changing events in our lives. Such an event could be the death of a family member, a serious illness, an accident, or the loss of a friend. These events are life changing because they are so significant that they have a lasting effect on an individual's values and perspective. Such events are most often unexpected and can plunge a person into a period of instability and confusion. Without warning, individuals can become victims of circumstances and feel a complete loss of control. New decisions must be made in one or more of the significant areas of their lives, the outcomes of which will affect their lives well into the future.

How individuals react during these difficult times can significantly impact how they will describe the lives they have had. Over the years, you may find yourself having to navigate crises and reassess all areas of your life to determine what, if any, adjustments need to be made. As you transition from one phase of life to another, you may want to seek assistance to help make the necessary decisions. Whatever the cause, these events present significant challenges and call for us to make thoughtful decisions and careful choices.

How do people in such periods of transition handle the instability and uncertainty? How much time do they let pass before they take action to recover from crises? The most distraught and depressed may feel overwhelmed and increasingly anxious as their fear of the future increases. They simply do not know how, or do not choose, to make the important decisions that are required to move forward. For some, the consequences of not working through this kind of transition can be more devastating than the event itself.

Moving Forward

We will all experience difficult periods in our lives, and the worst of those times will have the greatest impact on future decisions. Whether it is the loss of a relationship, a parent, or a job, you can regain control of your life by making decisions that will help you move forward. As difficult as that may sound, dwelling on the loss for too long will simply make it more difficult to get on with your life. We can learn from these significant emotional events if we view them as opportunities to reassess some of the life decisions we have already made. We may choose to develop new relationships, make changes to our living, school, or work environments, or reconsider career choices.

Ask adults to share their own significant moments, times when their lives were abruptly changed and they were forced to make new choices and find new directions. Whether by choice or out of necessity, when we take the time to reevaluate decisions we have made, we get closer to creating better lives for ourselves.

Questions to Think About

1. What, if any, life-changing events have you experienced in your life?

2. What new decisions did you need to make as a result of such events?

3. Did making new decisions help you to regain a feeling of control over your life? How and why?

Your Thoughts

_____
_____
_____
_____
_____
_____
_____
_____
_____
_____
_____

Things You Need to Do

_____
_____
_____
_____
_____
_____
_____
_____
_____
_____

IT'S YOUR DECISION!

Regardless of your age, whether you are in middle school or graduating from high school, choosing a college, searching for a job, or pursuing a career, the decisions you make have significant impact on the life you are creating.

Big-Ticket Decisions

It is not too soon for you to think about the big-ticket areas of your life. Which areas are most important to you right now? Are you satisfied with the decisions you have made in those areas? Did those decisions work out as you had hoped? Would change in any or all of those areas make you feel better about your life at this point? Now might be the perfect time to reconsider earlier decisions and make change happen.

Commitment to Learning

What kind of student are you? Are you a successful student? How much more education will you need in order to pursue the careers you are interested in? Education will be a major factor in determining what jobs and which careers will be available to you. Education gives you options and opportunities that you will not have without it. Identify the skills and knowledge that you will need in order to be successful in the career you choose. Then, make a commitment to yourself to get the training, certificate, or degree that you need to make the career a reality.

Whether you choose a career that is constantly changing or pursue a job that requires proficiency in technology, you will be able to keep your job only if you get the additional training and education that is needed to stay current in your field. It is most often the employees who stop learning who lose their jobs. They are seen as less committed, less knowledgeable, less skilled, and more expendable. Commit now to a life of learning, and you will realize greater opportunities for success.

Career Alternatives

Have you thought of some careers that sound exciting or challenging to you? If not, or if you have only identified a few, plan to do some more serious research. Search for job information on the Internet. Take an online interest inventory. Talk to your guidance counselor or to your teachers. When you see people doing jobs you might like to do, ask them about their work and their careers. They can share the pros and cons of their jobs, providing you with valuable insights. The sooner you can relate what you are learning in school to what you might want to do after graduation, the better student you will be. Education will help you reach your goals in work and in life. Of all of the decisions you make, now as a teenager and even later as an adult, those concerning your education will impact every one of the other areas of your life.

Your Relationships and Your Health

As a teenager, you are making decisions about who your friends will be and whom you choose to be significant in your life. You are giving thought to where you will want to live and work, how you want to spend your free time, and what kind of time and attention you will give to your health and well-being. The choices that you make in these and other big-ticket areas of your life will influence the overall quality of the life you have as an adult.

Start Today!

Start today to make better decisions as a teenager, and you will make better choices as an adult. As your responsibilities increase in the years to come, you will want to make decisions that will create opportunities to fulfill your needs and wants. *It's Your Decision (for Teens)* was written with one purpose in mind—to help teens understand the process and the power of good decision making. With practice, time, and effort, you learn how to make well-thought-out decisions in the big-ticket areas of your life. Challenge yourself to put together series of good decisions so that someday, when you look back and ask yourself, "What kind of life have I had?" you will be confident in answering "I have had a *great* life!" Remember, it's your decision!

Questions to Think About

1. What kind of a commitment have you made to being a successful student?

2. What careers have you researched?

3. Which of your relationships are the most significant in your life?

4. In what ways are you taking care of your health?

5. What are you doing to make the best use of your free time?

6. Of the big-ticket decisions you have made, which ones have had the best outcomes?

Your Thoughts

_____
_____
_____
_____
_____
_____
_____
_____
_____
_____
_____

Things You Need to Do

_____
_____
_____
_____
_____
_____
_____
_____
_____
_____

ABOUT THE AUTHORS

Al Foderaro and Denise Schmidt have offered counsel and advice to hundreds of students for more than thirty years. Having previously authored *It's Your Decision: A Commonsense Guide to Making Better Choices*, they are outspoken advocates for individuals taking control of their lives by making better academic, career, and personal decisions. They have encouraged and enabled teenagers and adults of all ages to make life's big-ticket decisions in ways that have produced favorable outcomes and positive results.

NOTES

NOTES

NOTES

NOTES

NOTES

NOTES

NOTES

NOTES